Quiet Talks with the Master

By
EVA BELL WERBER

DeVORSS & CO., *Publishers*
P.O. Box 550
Marina del Rey, CA 90291

Twenty-Eighth Printing, 1977

ISBN: 0-87516-104-9

Printed in the United States of America
BOOK GRAPHICS, INC.
Marina del Rey, CA 90291

FOREWORD

In moments of meditation these quiet talks were held with the Master of men. May they mean for each one who takes them unto himself a pathway into the secret of His Presence. They are sweet in fellowship, simple in language, yet they contain truths as vital as have ever been given down the ages to man.

"Keep and seek for all the commandments of the Lord your God."
I Chron. 28:8

CONTENTS

DEDICATED TO THOSE WHO

WALK THE PATH WITH ME

Quiet Talks With the Master

THE THRONE ROOM

MY CHILD, at the very center of your being there is a golden throne where Divinity dwells. Here you can come and meet your Lord in the quietness of your own soul. Come each day, my child set apart some special time; come, knock on that door of your heart and it shall swing open and you shall come in and hold sweet communion with the Lord of your Life.

I know, My child, it is often hard to steal away alone, the cares and duties of life press so closely and bind so surely; but if you will but try, if you will but make the effort, all these cares and duties shall fall into their proper relationship and you shall find such renewal of strength and beauty and calmness of spirit that as you leave that sacred spot and go again about the daily tasks you shall find every care lightened and the path of every duty made plain.

But, you say, how shall I find this throne room of my heart, how can I come close to this Divine Presence? And I say unto you, it is only by becoming very still that you can find the path, and when you find it the door shall open and flood your whole being with a glory of which you have never dreamed before. This being still does not mean a blank stillness, but rather a constant sense of inner quiet which you shall achieve when you have the firm knowledge that your God is in His Throne, not in some far off sky, but at the center of your own being.

And so you shall come to that Great Stillness, and there shall awaken in you the realization that you stand before a door that has long been closed and as you knock the door surely opens and you shall kneel before your Christ, sitting on the throne therein.

And so, day by day, I shall talk with you as we meet face to face. Each day shall a time be set apart to meet Me. I shall also be able to speak to you at other times and in many places if you will but tune your ear to the music of My voice; in the early morning when the world awakens to its loveliness; during the heat of the day when work must stop and you rest awhile by the roadside from life's activities; during the hour of sunset when shadows fall quietly over the land and the colors change and soften and the very air becomes calm and sweet with My Presence, and often again during the quiet darkness of the night you shall awaken, not in restless turning but to lie quietly and talk with Me.

So My Words shall fit every need as you journey on the path of peace, and you shall have a sense of fellowship and know that the hand of the loving Master of men holds your hand and leads you on and up, every step of the way.

THE CENTER OF BEING

I AM at the center of your being. I AM at the center of all the universe. As this thought becomes alive in your consciousness, all the power of it will flood your life. Live, My child, in this consciousness today and you shall be ready to receive other truths and lessons I would give you shortly. Each day shall you receive a message which shall be as a guidepost on the Path of Life.

THE CAUSE

I AM at the center of your being. I AM the cause of all that comes into your life. When sin, sickness or distress enter your being, it is because you have brought it there by ignoring My Perfect Law. You have followed a law of your own outward self, you have made it supreme and so receive that effect. The more you become conscious that the outward is only the expression of the within, and as you know and realize I AM at the center of your being, and that the outward is only the house wherein I dwell, to that degree of realization shall I be able to bring My Perfect Effect into evidence in your life. Carry with you this day this thought, I AM CAUSE, and the effects in your life shall be only such as glorify ME.

THE ABSOLUTE

I AM ABSOLUTE!

To see Me as the absolute in all lives, in your personal life, in the life of all things, whether plant, mineral, or animal is to come to the highest form of realization. Then you know that every cell, not only in your body, but in the universe, is a living, vibrant part of ME.

I AM ABSOLUTELY ALL THERE IS!

That which seems not of Me is only your mortal misconception. This full, complete realization is more than knowledge and does not come at once to you. So do not be dismayed if at times it seems only a hazy idea, but strive constantly to bring it more closely into your life's daily practice. Practice MY PRESENCE at all times and you shall thrill with the mighty rush of MY SPIRIT through you, as the canyon walls thrill and re-echo to the rush of the mighty waters rushing down between them. Go forth into the duties of your day, knowing I AM ABSOLUTE.

THE WARM PRESENCE

You have now had it shown to you that I AM CAUSE, and I AM ABSOLUTE. These terms seem cold and hard at times, but when you have fully mastered them, made them part of your life, you will know that I AM warm, vibrant and lovely within you. I radiate through your being as the warmth of the summer sun, as cool and refreshing as a mountain breeze, as calm as a starlit night, and as the sweetness of a flowering meadow.

So do not fear, My Child, that in seeing Me as Cause and Absolute that you will lose the sweetness of a friendly presence. You shall gain everything through that realization that makes life, both yours and the lives you contact, a gleaming reality.

Go now and carry the sweetness and warmth of MY PRESENCE with you.

YOUR ONLY GUIDE

Truly Beloved, your soul speaks to you. I AM leading you into many new experiences, and your only guide will be this My Inner Voice. So it is most necessary that you learn well to heed it. Know that every desire, every urge of your heart when you are listening for My Voice, will be My Desire; and if your life is full of My Desires, there will be no room for less worthy ones, and they will fade away as the mists fade before the sun. You wish to demonstrate and I tell you now that this is the only path of demonstration. Fill your life so completely with My Desires, My Thoughts, that I, the ABSOLUTE who created all things, will create through you, My Desire. It will seem perhaps to be a creation of your mortal mind, but never think of it as such. Know that you are but the instrument that I AM using to create physical things in a material world. Spiritual things in a spiritual world are created without the medium of a physical being. In bringing the spiritual essence into material being I must needs resort to the physical mediums which I have created. Therefore have every confidence as you image and give thanks for the physical manifestation of My Spiritual Idea, that you are only bringing into being that which I desire.

Go now, make the demonstration and know that in its fulfillment it shall be even as I decree.

BE STILL

Be still! Not as any stillness you have ever known before. The stillness which lies at the bottom of the ocean, eternally quiet, yet eternally vibrant and alive with infinite activity. Only by attaining this super-stillness can the full realization of former talks be attained. You must learn to keep this stillness, to retreat into it at any moment, whenever any confusion arises in your physical or mental world. Thus shall all difficulties solve themselves by My Power working through you. Learn to BE STILL instantly and watch God's Power work! In this potent stillness are all demonstrations made.

CONTACTING MYSELF

I have told you that in your being there is a throne where the I AM dwells. From that throne flow out all the life forces of your being and your existence. As those forces flow through you, I contact MYSELF in MY Universe, thus producing a complete harmony both in the within and the without. Learn to kneel often before that throne and drink of the power that reigns thereon. Thus shall My Power become your power to use in all your daily activities.

Only as you kneel before My Throne placing your human personality in entire subjection to My Divine Personality, can you be allowed to use My Power. It must be used only under My direction.

Carry this message with you through the day. Speak often to me. All that I have uttered shall be fulfilled and every word you utter shall be potent with My Power.

CHRIST LIVETH

My child, listen. Down the ages comes the echo, "Christ liveth!" The Christ has never died save in man's consciousness. Every day that you live oblivious to the Sweet Presence of My Spirit, I AM nailed to the cross of material things. Every moment that you open your heart and mind to My Inflow, the stone is rolled from your heart and the Christ ABSOLUTE in joy and beauty steps from the tomb, out into your daily life.

Thus is My Power released for all your daily needs, thus is My Power your power to use in demonstration, both for yourself and those I send to you for help. Then you will know that you do not choose whom you shall help or serve. I shall fill your life to such completeness that every step of the path will be of My Choosing and you have only to walk in it by faith to see My Glory revealed.

Go now, My child and know that Christ is risen indeed. Risen for you in a fuller sense than ever before and the tomb or cross shall never claim Him again in your consciousness. Make now your demonstration in the knowledge that He, Who is all Power, is with you walking by your side on the road.

THE PROTECTING LOVE

My child, I sometimes sense fear in your heart as you look ahead. You wonder what the unknown road will show to you. This need not and must not be. Remember that My Hand which is directing your way is the Hand of Divine Love. Those whom I direct as My channels to guide you shall only guide through Love. Sometimes there will be a checking-up and sharp commands, but that will only be as you falter and seem to linger too long on the way. So you see there is nothing to fear, never shall you be left alone, always a mantle of protecting love is thrown around you.

So My child, remember each day contains its lessons, and must contain its progress, and know that you are guided only by Divine Love.

"I am the Lord thy God, who teacheth thee to profit." Isa. 48:17.

THE COMMONPLACE DAY

Today has been an average day, you have gone about commonplace duties, you filled the hours with a needful *busyness*, yet all the while I was being expressed through you. The quick turning of a feeling of annoyance to a thought of compassion, was My Spirit moving into activity; the smile you gave even while wondering why you gave it, was the soul of your *be-ing* expressed. Always I am striving through you for expression, often in vain, but I give you these simple examples to show you how by listening to My Voice, by following your higher impulses you are enabled to express ME in every act of what you think a commonplace day.

So shall your life be enriched and the lives you contact, even as when a pebble is thrown into the water and the ripples travel on and on.

LIVING THE LESSON

You are just beginning to realize how difficult are My Lessons. Their language is simple and the thought seems plain and of easy understanding, but it is in the daily living in the constant realization of their reality that the problem is found.

Do not be discouraged when it seems utterly impossible to make these facts of My Dynamic Power an active ingredient in your life. Only by a more constant turning to Me within, will you be able to do this. Work steadily at it. Try each day to realize that I AM ABSOLUTE, which means All Power, All Supply, All Health, All Joy, All Sweetness, flowing constantly through and around you. You have many other lessons to learn but none will be greater than this. Until this is perfected in your life, the others must lie hidden from you. Press on, there is much to do and much to learn and the road is beautiful before you.

DEEDS NOT RESULTS

Let us talk quietly for a few moments. You are coming to see how I AM guiding and directing you every moment of your day. I AM sending to you those whom I desire you to help. Do not look beyond the moment of the helping or try to see the result; that is in the hands of your Father. It might give you joy to see the awakening and full flower of your work and in time it shall be so, but now you are to work in faith. It is one of the ways to grow, and part of the Divine Plan for you. As I see you are ready, I shall from time to time lift the veil and give you the greatest joy known—the joy of seeing the fulfillment of your work in My Service.

Go now, not seeking to see results, but to do deeds and ever shall you be guided to those who need a word of help and cheer. You are blessed to be chosen an instrument in My Creative Service.

MY DESIRES

My child, you have come to the end of your day, and ever have I guided you through its hours. You heard my voice and heeded it. Now as evening dusk lies over the land, and the gentle rain falls against the window, I can come very near to your consciousness, and you shall be able to know that the sweetness of My Presence drives away all darkness. If you will come now in faith, believing, to My Throne, I shall give to you of My richest treasures. I, the Absolute, speak through your mind, My Desires. Can I do other than answer My Own Call?

Ask now, fearing not. It shall be fulfilled. Come as to a Loving Father whose whole delight is to give good gifts to His children. And I say unto you, you shall not go unrewarded.

THE TREE

Let us talk quietly for a few moments. Still all outer thoughts and hear only My Voice, the Voice of the Silence. I would bring to you the vision of the Beautiful Tree. The tree is in full bloom and it represents your life and all lives. Your life shall become ever more like that lovely tree full of gorgeous blossoms. As you step out along the path and you keep your eyes ever on ME, know it is My Service in which you are enlisted. Guard well each word, thought and deed. In time your tree of life shall bear a golden harvest for Me. Thus shall you bring the tree of My Life into the hearts and souls of those who come under your ministry. Unless the blossoms of a tree partake of the sun and air and rain of God's heaven, they wither and die ere the time of fruitage. Even so, My child, you must partake of My Presence and My power and the Guidance I give you. Unless you do this, your tree of life, no matter how beautiful its blossoms, will fail to bear its full glory of fruit. So never feel that you are strong enough to walk alone, nor miss an opportunity for this quiet talk with Me, for unless I guide you, the blossoms will fall and work which has been done shall have to be done over and over again.

Again and yet again shall your life have to be brought to the time of blossoming until you know how to carry on to the place where it will bear the golden fruit. My child, I AM ever near to you and My Helpers stand nearby to guide your footsteps on the Path of Peace and Service.

TALK TO ME

Tenderly and softly do I speak to you. You shall talk more freely to Me, learn to speak to Me of the problems and things which seem to disturb your mortal mind. You carry these things too much alone. They sap your vitality and hinder your progress and the ability to hear the voice in your soul. Each morning as you sit at my feet, bring with you all the perplexities of the moment, whether of greater or lesser importance. Speak freely to me of them, for no one else is so close to you and these problems as I am at the heart center of your Being.

You have learned to be quiet that I may talk to you. Now you must learn to talk to Me. Then after this sweet communion together you will be able to put away all disturbance and go forth wearing the armor of the Christ Consciousness, with a mind clear and open to the highest influences. Heed well, My child, these words, for they shall be vital to you in coming days.

BRING YOUR BURDENS

This day I would bring you a new message which contains a key to many things. I have told you how you must learn to talk to Me. As you come each morning in quiet humbleness to the door of the golden throne room of your heart, the door swings wide for you and you enter as a weary pilgrim, carrying your dust-covered burdens that you have gathered along life's highway. As you kneel before My Presence on the throne take from your heart one by one, these burdens. Some shall seem almost too small and trivial to have made so large a bundle, and so recently acquired that you wonder at its weight upon you. Others you may have carried long, and these will be bound by the very fibers of your heart. But never fear, My child, they are all burdens in My Sight.

Anything, no matter how small, that fetters the soul, must be taken from your shoulders. So give them all to Me. Talk them over with Me. Say, "My Lord and King, this may seem small, but it bothers and hinders me. Take it, that I may be free." And then as these burdens whether great or small (and the "small" shall always by far exceed the "great" in number) are given over into My Keeping, they shall immediately be consumed by the Holy Fire on My Altar, and you shall stand straight and free in My Presence.

You entered the throne room through a wide open door as a mortal carrying a heavy burden. When you leave, the door remains closed and you go out as a free spirit. No burden can go through that closed door into the outer again, and the fragrant incense of My Altar Fires will cling to your garments and you shall all the day walk among your fellowmen with the Signs of My Presence upon you.

GO FORTH FREE

You shall learn in time to come often to the throne room. You shall not wait and come only when you have gathered many burdens, for while you are on the plane of motral thought you will always acquire burdens, and small annoying things are among the common lot. But you will learn to come often through the wide open door and to talk to ME of things which seem constantly to disturb you. The door is always open when you come, but always closed when you leave. Remember, no burden is too large nor small to bring to My Presence, but none can be taken away. You shall come quietly into My Pressence, but you will leave, singing prayers of thankfulness that you go forth a free spirit.

You say, "Lord, suppose I feel again the weight of the same old burden; it may be hard for me to recognize that I do not still have it upon my heart." At first it may seem so, but as you come, again and again, fettered, and go forth free, it will come into your consciousness that it is only the memory of the old burden which you carry away with you, and the time will not be long until even the memory shall not go through the closed door. And as these things are taken from you and your mind is left serene and open to My Voice and My Influence, you will find that all affairs of your outer life will fall into the rhythm of My Step and a harmony such as you have never dreamed possible shall possess your being. Let us work together, my child, as two who are indeed one. Let us talk together. Come to Me as My Beloved, for I would have you free — free for My creative work, free to grow and blossom and bear fruit in My service. Go now, but come often and talk to Me, for I have things to tell you as you draw close to Me in the sweet peace of My Sanctuary in your heart.

GIVE FREELY

I want you to live with the message I have just given you. It is so vibrant with My Truth that it shall be made a very part of your Being. There are many other truths I have for you, but I give them only as former lessons are learned. Too much given too rapidly is like giving a child to much sweet. My child, blessed art thou that we can talk together, that not only your life but many lives may be enriched.

As you hark back, you have come a far step in consciousness, but yet you are at the beginning of the path. Such riches I have in store for you as we journey on, your hand in mine! I give joyously to one who is so eager to receive. I long to give and shall, just as fast as you are able to bear the glory of the gifts. My child, bow your head, that My Hand may rest upon it in blessing, ere you go forth with Me into the duties of the day before you.

FLOOD OF GOLDEN SILENCE

Listen quietly to Me. My child, as you enter the golden throne room of your innermost Being, as you kneel before Me on the throne of your Consciousness it is not always necessary that words pass between us. Often I would treat you in a flood of golden silence. As that sacred spot takes on the glory of My Presence, it takes on a peace and purity of which the human mind cannot conceive. I would wrap you in these vibrations. With My Hand on your bowed head I would have you absorb this high glory. I can give you in the deep silence a golden glow which you shall wear as an armor all the day and which nothing but love will penetrate. You often feel a weight upon you, you know not why nor whence it comes. That I can wash away by this Pure Radiance. So you see that these trysts which you keep so faithfully are threefold. There is the Father, who like the loving earthly father, gives you gifts of health, plenty, and fullness of all things. Greatest among these, the gift of the Son, who takes from your heart all burdens, bearing them in his holy hands to the golden flame of the altar fires, setting you free from all limitations. This same Father-God, gives to you the Holy Spirit, which in the depth of that great Silence, floods every atom of your Being with a Holy Fire of Divine Vibration. Then you are as a golden string on the harp of your Lord. From this three-fold tryst you go forth into the world of men a bearer of gifts from the Father, free from your burdens through the Grace of the Son and bathed in a fire of Righteousness by the Holy Spirit.

Thus does the Holy Trinity take its place in your life and in the lives of others.

GUIDING HANDS

There are certain things of which I would speak to you this morning, My child. You often feel a mental confusion as if you were in a dark room groping for a light which you cannot find. But listen, he who seeks, always finds. No soul is so hopelessly lost in darkness as is that soul which feels it has all the light. There are many graduations of light, and no matter how much you have, there is always more for you to acquire. Some light no man can give you; it must come only from ME at the center of your being. But guiding hands can help you and shall be directed to do so. Do not fear; remember I have told you, I AM by your side and I walk and talk with you on the path. Can He who planned the order and rhythm of the great cosmic universe of which you are a part, bring aught but order into that life which is directed so closely by Him?

Live each moment today under My Direction and I promise you light on the path and help along the way. Nothing which comes into your life is chance. Follow Me. I direct and choose the Way for you and I direct guiding hands on both the earth and spiritual planes to help and sustain you. Be still,

put aside all thoughts of your own, and let the
leaven of My Spirit work through you.

RICHES OF THE SOUL

You have brought to Me the things which bother
you, and placed them in My Hands that they may
be consumed in My Holy Flame. You came with
them on your heart and as they were taken from
you, they were always replaced with rich gifts of
the spirit. You shall not only go forth from My
Presence without the burdens, but you shall go forth
enriched with My rich gifts of spiritual things. Where
the Spirit of the Lord is, there are riches indeed.
These riches of the soul are of far more worth
than precious gems, gold or silver. They fill your
life with such an overflow of peace and love that
all your day is made lovely thereby. All your contacts are contacts of joy and loveliness.

Can you not see, My child, the harm you do
not only to yourself, but to all of your world,
when you carry for one moment a burden, whether
great or small? As you seem to pick them up along
the highway, and they cling like tenacious burrs
to your garments, quickly, Oh so quickly, give them
to Me, that they may be replaced by one of My
rich gifts for you. This is the meaning of My An-
cient Words, My people should "rejoice in tribu-

lation." Yes, rejoice in it, because I take it from you and for every trial removed there comes a blessing. My child, so many golden truths I long to disclose to you and shall as the time seems right. Now wait quietly for the deepest inner blessing and then go forth safely and securely into the day before you.

THE HOLY READJUSTMENT

I would speak further with you regarding the burdens which you bring to Me to be lifted from your heart and consumed by the Altar Fires. The question arises in your mind, "Lord, can they just be consumed, and thus leave my life? What of their effects, how shall taking the fear of them from my heart solve the problem?" Listen, carefully, My child, for this is the kernel at the heart of the message. It is only the fear and the weight of the burden, the outer wrappings, that are burned at the altar. This leaves the heart of it exposed to the rays of My Divine Intelligence and Wisdom. This washes and purges it in a holy readjustment. Unseen, but mighty Forces take this heart out of the problem and work it out on the basis of My Truth and My Perfect Harmony. Readjustment in the outer life must and shall follow, as daylight follows night. So you see, My Beloved, there is never cause for fear, *never* are you justified in carrying for one moment a thing which distresses you.

You shall put this to the test and find it true. Now you have a deeper understanding of how My Love operates when you do your part and accept the great privilege, which is so freely given. You understand now how you really have a right to go forth from this tryst, free in every way for My Service. Knowing this, if you are still fettered by anything, whether great or small, it shall displease and grieve Me greatly. Your mind must ever be open and receptive to My Truths. They cannot penetrate a mind distraught by outer disturbances. Peace and the secret of Peace I have now given you. Go forth and practice it!

PETTY BURDENS

My child, come for a few moments, for a quiet talk. You are finding each day how easy a thing it is to bring all your problems to Me. You are also finding how small most of them are. Each day they seem to gather. By no law shall man be free from gathering these petty burdens, but you will find as you constantly turn to Me, following the plan I have given you, that larger problems and greater distressing things shall have no place in your life. As small weeds of worry and fret are kept out of your mental garden, the rhythm of your life will be so in tune to My Divine

Rhythm, that all your affairs shall flow smoothly and in true law and order. So, as I have told you before, it is of uttermost importance that every smallest thing be brought to Me, that it may be readjusted according to My Law.

COMPLETENESS WITHIN

Come, let Me speak to you for a moment. You feel often a restlessness and sense of aloneness. This comes to you that you may turn to the God-*Mother* within you and find completeness. More and more shall you learn the valuelessness of the outer and the great Power of the Inner. Do not let these days of seeming restlessness disturb you. I know it is hard, but you must learn that then of all times is the time to be still. Though you may seem not to hear My Voice, yet know It is speaking to you through the silent depths of your soul and that soon the shafts of My Sunlight shall penetrate through the fog of the outer mind and My Peace shall be in your heart. So never fail at such a time to contact Me, for of what value can I be to you unless I can serve when you need Me most?

PROBLEMS

There are other things of which I shall speak to you this morning besides the burdens, and little

annoying things which each life contains. These I
have shown you how to dispose of and you must
needs spend much time in the practice of that all-
important lesson. Now I would speak to you concerning perplexing problems, of which every life
must have its share. Often there comes not one,
but many of these and you wonder at the way they
confound you. They are alike, yet different, from
the burdens and cares. Alike in that they keep
your mind working on outer things and conditions,
and disturb the deep inner communion I would
have with you. They are unlike in that there is
something more for you to do about them. They
are given you for a different purpose and brought
by a different cause. But, My child, they are also
alike in that they can be brought to Me in the
throne room of your heart. Come, place them all
before Me, place them with the burdens and wor-
ries and cares in My hands. We shall talk them
over together. Possibly of some I shall say, "It is
not really a problem at all, My child. Leave it
entirely with Me and I will take it from your life
and heart." Some which you think are cares, I
will show to you as problems. I shall say, "Let us
talk this over a little more fully." I shall want
your help in this, for this is given that you may
learn to choose, to use good judgment. If I took it
entirely out of your hands you would not grow.
Your outer mind must develop as well as your
spiritual mind. To be perfect in My Service you

must be well rounded and developed in every way.

I shall give you more of this in the next lesson. Come now, with all these things and I will show you how I can help you in every way that your life may be free for My Service.

THE CALM MIND

My child, we were talking together of problems which come into a life and which must need be untangled, thought out and worked through. As these problems and questions arise in your outer experience, never forget for a moment that within is the mind of Christ. Do not waste time in idle speculation or thinking but come within for quiet contemplation with the Master of your Soul. Thus can you make Him not only your soul's Master, but Master of all outward conditions.

As you lay the problem before the Christ-Mind within, as you talk it over in every phase of its perplexities, as you say, "Lord I don't know how to decide this thing, I cannot see the future, or know what will be best in coming days," there will come a quiet peace, which will leave the outer mind so hushed and still, so calm, that it will reflect the inner mind as a lovely lake reflects the reality of the trees on its banks. Then the thoughts and ideas which come to you concerning that which is so confounding will be clear, all-compelling, definite, that you will know the way to take. All outer circumstances shall so evolve themselves, and work together, that there will be found only one course which you would consider taking; and with the peace and feeling of sureness within your whole being, you will know that this is My Choice for you. From this point of higher knowledge and consciousness, you have used your freedom of choice and chosen My Way to solve your problem.

So you are free, unfettered, a soul standing upright, using all of your God-Given Powers. Then are you really open for further growth and development. There are many hidden truths and meanings in these last lessons. Ponder them, study them! They are given you as a compass to chart your day's activities, and only as they are made use of shall you be given more and more of My Wisdom. Only by living with them can you in turn pass them on to other souls, whom I would have receive them from you.

SWEET COMMUNION

My child, you have felt and experienced a reality of My Presence such as you have never known before. This sense of My Loving Presence shall grow greater each day as you study and ponder the words I have spoken to you from time to time. You have earthly contacts which are rich in spiritual value, which bring to your soul an uplift and which enable you to walk more firmly upon the path. This is well and I have planned it so. Always as you meet others who are walking the way, will you feel a sense of peace and harmony. But these contacts are but a reflection of the I AM Who is the CAUSE and ABSOLUTE, at the heart center of your being.

So can you not see when you go to the throne within your own heart, all the peace and loveliness of the sweetest communion is yours instantly? Come, My child, really know Me as I long to be known by you. Not that only your life may be blessed, but that all lives you contact may be enriched by My Consciousness. I must needs be more and more manifest in My Universe, and only by the pure reflection through you and others who are close to Me, can I be brought into the outer expression which I must needs have.

Never fail to re-study the lessons previously given, for unless they are made an active part of your life, My Reflection would indeed be most imperfect. Let us travel the path together, My child, today, and I shall show you what glories can shine through commonplace things and simple, everyday living.

THE RADIANCE OF MY PRESENCE

This morning I bring you a lesson I have longed to give you. As you come to My Throne, as you meet Me there, not only as the Lord of your being but as the loving, tender Friend of your heart, you find that you need not go into detail over the things you wish to place in My Hands to solve for you. You now know that by just breathing the thought, I understand. Why and how? Because I AM truly closer to you than your breath. Even affirmations shall begin to seem unnecessary to you, for I shall grow more and more to be a very personal part of you. Your faith will be so strong and you will feel such an overwhelming flow of My Love for you whenever you turn to the throne within, that all your conscious speaking to Me shall be given over to rejoicing and praise for the Radiance of My Presence in your heart and life. Do you not see, My Beloved, that as long as you feel the necessity to beseech Me, to plead with Me by affirmations, or to contact Me by any method whatever, there is in some degree a sense of separateness in our relationship?

But when you come with the knowing that all things that bother and hinder and puzzle you, are even in that moment that you step into the throne room, instantly absorbed by the rays of My Divine Love, you shall find as you enter My Presence you enter rejoicing and praising that you are already free from all things from which your soul should be freed.

I gave first the lesson of bringing each burden and telling Me of it and asking its release and destruction, asking My help in solving the problem.

But even as I gave it, I knew it was but a stepping-stone on the way to attainment. As you fulfilled that law, as you so practiced My Presence, so surely would come this higher attainment of which I speak this morning. And so, My child, old things shall pass away in the inner life, as well as the outer, and always shall you go on and up the golden pathway to My Throne. So shall My Power flow from your very garments, so shall you walk and talk with Me and your own personal life will become only a mirror of that which is within your soul.

ONENESS

Truly, My child, we are One indeed, yea One in all things whatsoever. Can you not now see that by a more constant attainment of this conscious Oneness with Me, you have not only learned but taken into your very life substance the lessons I have given you? You are a very part of the Great Life, and in seeing Me as the ABSOLUTE you see the cause of all things having its effect in every phase of your life, both physical and spiritual. You begin to find that the golden throne room of your heart is not a place merely to come to now and then, as the world presses closely about you; not a place only to bring the burdens and problems that you may be freed from them; or again, to find My Altar Fires, that you may warm yourself thereby; — but it shall gradually come to be the only spot in your life where reality prevails. It shall be your very dwelling. Constantly shall you have the benefit of the Rays of My Presence, for listen, My Beloved One, as you know that nothing can separate you from Me, that in essence you *are* Me, you will fully know that it is impossible to withdraw one moment from My Presence on the throne.

As long as your life shall last, and knowing that life has no beginning and no ending, do you not see the meaning of the words, "Nothing can separate us from the Love of God?" As you take up this complete realization of your Oneness with Me, there shall follow the knowledge and consciousness of your Oneness with all your fellowmen and the resultant harmony therewith.

So shall you count all men your brothers, and those who are yet stumbling in darkness. But you, by your higher consciousness shall be able to hold a light aloft for other members of My Body who have yet to attain to the knowledge which you now have. You shall likewise be permitted to gain knowledge from souls who have received much of My Light and there shall therefore be a perfect circuit of interchanging helpfulness for all of My Creation. There is a great depth of meaning in this lesson. Study it for many days and it shall indeed light the way before you.

THE ARMOR

You must learn from this day to shield from yourself all destructive thoughts and influences. You must learn to draw an armor about yourself, to say quickly when annoying things arise, "This cannot touch me, I am wearing the armor of Christ Consciousness." Practice this faithfully and see with what safety and calmness you will be able to move among your daily contacts. You are in the world, yet above its tumult; calm and still within, for nothing but good can penetrate the shining armor of the Christ.

My child, the restlessness within your soul is as a bird, beating its wings against the bars. Your soul is beating against the bars of the material for the full revelation of My Truth.

THE VISION AHEAD

Come, receive your message for the day, and know these are indeed My Words. The path on which I lead you is straight and narrow. The vision lies ahead. True, there seem to be beauties along the roadway; others there are who you will feel can give you strength, can tell you how to walk the path; but listen carefully to Me, only the Great I AM of your soul shall you follow. True it is that you shall be given help and guidance by other of My Beings; but these, the teachers to whom the task shall be given, are not found beside the path, but ahead on it. Others who come after you, you too shall help, but only as you keep your eyes straight ahead and feet firmly planted, can you help these, My Little Ones, to point their feet in the right direction.

Three words I give you this day which shall be words of living power to you, which shall break down all barriers before you, and which shall light every step of the way. They are WATCH, PRAY, LISTEN! They shall be words of living power to you which shall break down all barriers and light every step of the way.

WATCH! Watch your spoken words, knowing they are all-powerful; and they will bring their effect into your life. WATCH, knowing that by word and thought you can rule the kingdom of your heart and all outer conditions.

PRAY! Give thanks for the power of your spoken word. Give thanks that you are guarded on the path. Give thanks for the great silent helpers who tread the King's Highway with you. Pray in humbleness for more light to recognize these helpers and know they are of Me. Pray in humbleness to recognize My Constant Direction in your life and the lives you contact.

In the babble of earthly things, LISTEN. Listen, be still. Do not lose My Voice with Its lovely Melody. *Be still,* that Its beauty may seep into your consciousness, that the radiant rays of My Spirit may warm your very Soul's fires. Listen to the music of My Spheres. Listen to the rhythm of My Footsteps and the swish of My Garments on the path. Then shall no inharmonious sounds break the beauty of Our Meditations as you journey with your hand in Mine, And so again, I give you the three words, not for this day alone, but for every day.

WATCH! PRAY! LISTEN!

MY PLAN

My child, I have longed to speak to you regarding many things which have pressed hard upon you, these last days. Only by keeping close your contact with Me, can you survive some of the earth conflicts and retain through it all your Christ Consciousness. Come, let us be still together. A new day lies ahead, will you walk the path with Me? Still all outer confusion, cease all foolish planning, let Me help you. Let My plans work through you. When it is hard to know what My Plan is for you to follow, *stand still*, wait, and when I say, "Step forward," then go in full assurance that it *is* My Plan for you. Never shall I give a problem too great to solve by the light of My Consciousness, never a cross or burden that you cannot carry with My Help. Often, My child, you must meet the testing, again and again shall you be tried, until you come where you shall never leave the Consciousness of My Presence no matter what comes or goes in your outer experience. I AM with you. I AM your very Being. Today, turn constantly within and I will direct every action, every word. Study, dwell upon past lessons, and when twilight comes, with it shall come a Peace that passeth all understanding. You shall know that I AM truly the Only One within. I AM causing all things in your life to work according to Law for you. Do not feel as you leave this tryst that you leave Me. How can you leave what is so a part of you? Rather know that in a loving Comradeship, we go forth together to meet the problems of the day.

"Yet the Lord will command His Loving Kindness in the daytime, and in the night His song shall be with me and my prayer unto the God of my life." Ps. 42:8.

RENEWED VIGOR

You come to me this morning feeling in your heart that you have not lived as close to Me as you should, that there is a richness of Spirit which somehow you have failed to receive in the past days. But do not grieve, it is ever so. Always shall you look up and long for more of My Grace and Loveliness in your life. Yet at times, with all your knowledge and all your desires, against all the higher impulses of your soul, you seem to withdraw yourself from Me, from the constant realization of My Presence. I allow this to be so, My child, that when you return, coming again to kneel at My Altar in the Throne Room of your heart, you shall find such renewed vigor and sweetness and light, that each time returning thus, you shall find it easier to abide at all times in My Presence.

So do not be discouraged. I understand. I, Who am never separated from you, only by your own lack of recognition of Me, understand how easy a thing it is to allow the world to come in and close the golden room of your heart, shutting out the light of your soul. Now, my child we shall take up anew these lessons. We shall walk and talk together, and you shall find that new joys and new happiness, new duties, will follow, as you walk consciously with the Master of Your Soul.

GIVE THANKS

I would reveal to you a secret, whereby you can bring all things under your feet, and stand conqueror over all circumstances. It is the secret of giving thanks, constantly. Rejoice, give thanks, praise! For every circumstance, in every move of your life, lift your heart in thanksgiving. Thus you release My Power into your life and link yourself with these Great Forces. For in the true heart-lifting thanksgiving — not just the mumbling of words—you reach that faith which removes mountains. Can you give thanks for what you have not? As you give thanks you know you have, and you *do* have.

Look about you, see how much you have which you accept so casually. When you know it is of Me, give your praise to Me, and you shall realize how much you have of My Goodness and Protection, and to him who hath, shall be given! Practice this and see what miracles shall take place for you. Now, My child, the day's duties lie before you; walk with Me and they shall be made light.

STEPS

"The steps of a good man are ordered of the Lord." Think, My child, on the word, "steps." I truly order each step. I do not devise a plan and then leave you in your human weakness to work it out alone. No, each moment of the day I direct and guide and order. Always am I by your side, My Hand in yours, leading out and on and upward, so you do not have to ask, "Lord, what am I to do all week? Give me Your plan." No, you only have to say, "Lord show me what to do now, this moment. Show me how to solve this problem which confronts me."

If you will learn this lesson well, you shall never look with fear or uncertainty into future days, you shall fear neither lack of material things nor spiritual guidance, for you will know, oh so surely, that each step of the way is guided and planned, and that you do not walk, even for one moment, life's highway alone.

YOUR WORK

Come, My child, let peace be in your heart this day. Abide close to Me and have no thought or fear for future days. Many new experiences lie just ahead of you. In the soon-coming days you shall realize as you do not now, how far you have traveled on the path. Listen carefully to these words; your work begins now — not in some future time as you are apt to think, but even now is service required of you. You will grow from now on, by service. It shall not always be of your choosing, sometimes you may not even recognize it as a service to Me, but it is all planned, and you have a very definite place in the work which must go rapidly forward.

You are learning to love the quiet of eventide, the quiet of the mountain top, the quiet of dim-lit churches. All things that are sweet and lovely and still, your soul responds to as never before. It is as I choose, for then you hear My Voice, then can I reach the innermost paths of your being and show you My Way and direct your steps. Oh My Beloved, seek every opportunity to be with Me; then shall the world and its bitter strife and loud clamor have no effect upon you, for you shall be abiding in the secret place of the Most High and learning the secrets of the Sanctuary of Your Lord.

LOVE AND BEAUTY

I AM LOVE and I AM BEAUTY. I sent forth My Thought when I created My Universe. I loved that which I created, henceforth there came forth Beauty. All the elements, which are but My Forces, caused beauty to evolve. All My Creations are beautiful and breathe forth My Love.

My child, do you not see, that as you are more and more attuned to Me, only love shall be the prime factor in your life? And as this is so, there shall be only beauty. All aspects of your life shall be beautiful, yea not only the spiritual, but also the material, for it is all a part of the Divine Life.

The life which is asleep to My Consciousness is like to one passing through the blank darkness of a tunnel. There is no beauty, light, nor form; only a mere flat, blank existence. You, My child, know so well the glories of a life awakened to Me, and as you go about touching other lives, you shall open a way out of the tunnel for them. You shall not always be conscious of doing this, but as you radiate Me, it cannot help but be so and every life will become more beautiful and more love-filled as you contact it along your upward way.

MY RADIATION

Come, My daughter, I have placed you where you now are. No step of your way is unconsidered in My Plan for you. Formerly your way was self-chosen to a great extent, but now it is Spirit-chosen and guided. You need have no fear. As long as you are consciously about your Father's business, shall you not have the Father's protection and guidance?

You are touching many lives, lives in all degrees of consciousness, each with its individual problems, yet each a part of My Body. Can you not feel how I yearn over Mine Own? And you, My child, as My Ambassador, go up and down not always conscious of how I AM radiating through you, touching these other of My children who are so deadened to Me, soothing, healing, blessing, coming close to them. You have but to lift your consciousness in blessing as you pass and know that the Father indwelling doeth the work. Fill your life so full of My Presence that never for a moment shall you fail to allow Me to radiate through you.

You shall find others more and more seeking and desiring your presence. In darkness they think it is your personal self they desire to be near.

But you know that you are only a mirror for My Face, and it is I whom they feel through you that causes them to turn to you. You, yourself will receive many blessings, as you know this truth; but only as you keep self down, recognizing it is the Christ they seek. Only as you touch these lives with Love and silent blessing, laying aside all thought of personal gain, shall you be a fit instrument for Me.

Many obligations rest upon you, as you so serve Me. Your life is no longer your own in the old sense, yet in the coming days you shall feel a freedom such as you have never known before, for you walk the King's Highway as a child of the King. You can know no want, either material or spiritual, for your Father who has created all things, gives all things freely for your use.

PEACE AND HARMONY

My Beloved, as you look upon My Universe, as you see the beauty of My creation, you find it good. You find harmony in the music of My winds as they play among the tree-tops. My sun and My shadows rest softly upon the land I have created for your use. There is a perfume in the air, and a gentle peace in all My Handiwork. When you take your eyes from these things, and descend onto the plane of mortal endeavor, you find discord, strife, antagonism, harsh words, cruel deeds. How different from the plane where you meet the King of the throne room of your heart. Truly while you are in the body, and living the mortal life you needs must deal with the plane of mortal thought. Every moment that you can use to escape into the higher realm with Me, the Lord of your being, you shall do, for only by this constant contact with Me can you walk in the midst of men and mortal things, with the serenity of a child of the Christ. Only through you and others of My enlightened ones, can the Christ Spirit be brought to the earth plane. Close your eyes at any moment and contact Me, and drink of My Fountain of Peace and Harmony.

FINDING ME

My child, you ask for service. Verily shall it be given. All about you shall you find it. You so little realize the Great Power flowing through you. You are like a mighty dynamo, and more and more shall you see miracles rise up as you pass on your way.

Only *Love* much, bless, and give thanks, and know you serve Me day by day as I see fit.

You cry out for light and understanding, and you cry not in vain. Great truths shall be revealed to you; listen for My Voice, that these things shall not pass you by. You often feel a need to find Me in ceremonies, in rituals. I feel a crying-out in your soul for some way to contact Me. But listen carefully and ponder much on this — a truth which many lose, and which keeps them from the companionship with Me which otherwise they might have. It is this: In simple ways and by simple means is the best contact made between man and his Maker. You need not seek out places where altar fires burn, or go through deeply impressive ceremonies. Light the altar fires in the throne room of your heart and there shall you find Me, and know Me, through the simple everyday things in life, all about you. Yes, I AM even now in the gentle breeze you hear through the rustling leaves. I AM in the shaft of sunlight slanting across the grass. I AM in the fragrance of the flowers, in the starry sky and the soft moonlight. Learn to know Me through these simple, lovely things of My Creation, and never shall you have need to seek Me out in complex ways. So blest art thou to hear My Voice in the inner thoughts and recesses of your soul, My child, as I bring you these truths. You can serve Me well, for they are as a foundation stone for a life lived in My Service.

YOU WALK AT ONE WITH ME

My child, I come to you this morning as a loving tender friend. I, who walked the hills of Galilee, who walked and talked with multitudes, yet was so often alone—yea, lonely, for even those whom I loved did not understand. And so I know your heart and the loneliness of it. Those to whom you have looked for years, for friendship and understanding, often seem to satisfy no longer. But My daughter, I say to you now, when this feeling assails you, turn within and find the Peace of My Presence. You cannot reach your goal or do your work, and carry with you the baggage of worldly friends and acquaintances. The path is narrow, but the goal lies ahead. You must needs tread much of it alone with your Lord.

But listen now, dry the tears of your heart, for I AM going to speak to you that which shall never fail to give you comfort. When you reach the place where you now are, when you say, "Lord, it is dark and lonely, where are those with whom I have walked?" then shall you know that you have gone far on the path and that in the moment when you realize your aloneness with Me, know that you shall receive help. My Helpers, seen and unseen, are by your side and by this very aloneness you have opened the way for their ministry. Peace My child, in your heart and know that I, your Lord, it is who leads you on.

OUTER MANIFESTATION

You shall find, as time moves on and you keep sacred the tryst with Me, that whatsoever is good which you hold in your heart, shall be brought into outer manifestation. From day to day your thoughts shall create and bring forth after their kind. Be sure that they are My Thoughts, that I may bless their coming into outer form. And now, blessings on you, you have truly learned the way of life everlasting. The way to true living will be found as you rest yourself by the roadside and talk with Me, the Giver of all Life. Then shall you go out to the contacts with the busy world, refreshed and made whole, ready for any service to which I shall lead you. Sometimes you shall only have a moment to pause, ere you go your busy way, for My Blessing, but even a quick turn of the heart to Me at any time or place will heal and bless, for lo, I AM with you always, and there is no spot where I AM not known.

THE OPEN CHANNEL

And now, My child, you say you are an open channel for My Healing Forces. These are words of truth, but not only shall the channel be open to the healing Christ inflow, but it must be a worthy channel. As the channel is freed for My Entrance, freed of selfishness, narrowness, bigotry, lust, evil of all kind, it must also be filled with their opposites—love, unselfishness, an impersonal attitude, meekness, truth, honesty. All the fruits of the spirit must blossom there. Then and indeed then only, can the perfect inflow take place. Then and then only shall the perfect healing come.

You say, "Lord, how can I become thus, and have daily contacts and live in a world which does not conform to these standards?" But I say, "Be of good courage, each day shall you go a little further on the path of attainment." Each day shall you look back from the mountain heights and see below the path you have trod. I only ask that you try, that you commune with Me. I accept the earnest desire of your heart for My Perfect Life, and through that desire, you are healed.

MY FLAME IN YOUR HEART

As the golden flame of the candle burns steadily, without flicker or wavering, so shall My Flame burn ever more in your heart. It shall burn out all dross of the mortal mind, smallness of nature, meanness of spirit, vindictiveness, jealousy. It shall burn out all carelessness of your habits, in the outer realms of your being. My Law and My Order then can function perfectly in your life. Then and then only will you be a worthy vessel for the inflow of My Spirit. Then and then only can My Spirit flow through you to other of my children.

Likewise shall all disease be burned from the physical body, that nothing shall interfere with My Plan for your life. As the sigh of your Spirit disturbs the flame and makes the candle drip, so the faintest wavering of your feet from the path of attainment causes a less steady burning of My Flame in your heart, and My work goes on in imperfection. Oh, My Beloved, how necessary that you live with the eye single, to the high purpose of your calling. But you have many helpers. No soul who enters the path is left to walk alone. So go on, day by day, with the light and assurance of My Love in your face. Mighty Ones whom you see not, are by your side. And the forces of darkness shall touch you not.

PERFUME OF MY PRESENCE

Let us again resume our quiet talks. One such moment, spent at My feet shall carry you farther on the path than hours spent searching for Me in books. I have told you, yea now I command again, cease from wandering, and come direct to Me, and learn in simple ways how to go far in My Service. Fill yourself with the sweet perfume of My Presence. Come, know the Inner Secrets of the Heart of your Lord.

Oh, My child, such glories would I show you, such marvelous things would I make known to you, but only can I speak through a mind that is single. Be not afraid for your progress. Do not try to interpret, through writings, My Law for you, for after all, if you busy yourself to know the Law and keep it not, wherein lies the profit? It is well! Come again as a little child, for as such have I guided you thus far down the path which leads to the freedom and glory of your soul.

A SIMPLE RITE OF LIVING

My Beloved, let us hold sweet communion for a little space, quietly apart from the noise and hurry of life's activities. I know only too well that it is hard to hear the Inner Voice, when the noise and rush of life is all about you, but listen, and take heart. Every impulse for a thoughtful act, every single smile given from a heart filled with love, not only for the loved ones of your own, but for all humanity, every kind word spoken, when the hasty word would have come so much easier, is proof that all unconsciously you have allowed Me to direct your footsteps. And a day thus spent, when evening shadows quietly fall, shall find you further on the path, walking step by step with your Lord. So do you not see, My child, it is not a greatly complicated thing to journey on the path to attainment? It is after all just a simple rite of living, recognizing My Consciousness in all whom you contact, and knowing after all, even though you recognize it not, you are hearing every moment of the day My Voice.

A PART OF THE CHRIST BODY

Know so truly these words, "I and the Father are One." There are so many creeds, so much dogma, it is all made so complex a thing — this walking the path with Me. And that is why I would have you show My children how simple a thing it can be to come as a little child and sit quietly with Me for a little while, letting Me speak from the inner depths of your being, telling you the way to the fullness of life lived in My Consciousness.

You long for development and work for Me. Be not so fearful, step out, that I the Lord of your soul may lead you into yet greater and larger ways. Of yourself you are nothing. Only by a recognition of yourself as a part of the Christ Body, as a part of the whole unit, can your life and work be acceptable to your Lord. Be very still, that the inner depths of your soul may be renewed through the Power of My Spirit.

THE SEA OF ABUNDANCE

My Beloved, truly all that the Father hath is yours. Not tomorrow, not in some far off heaven, not after you have struggled to attain, but *now*, this moment, you are in a vast sea of abundance, abundance for all your need. Do you need health, money, friends, wisdom, learning? Yea, you are living not only surrounded by it, but literally infused with it.

Therefore listen carefully, heed well these words, for by them was the world created. You have no need, for all is instantly yours. The merest suggestion of need in the outer consciousness shall be instantly met with an inner consciousness of fullness of supply; and I say unto you, in that moment, quicker than your next breath, God's forces are put into motion and the need is dissolved in the great Ocean of My Abundance, even before it was ever conceived. And so, My child, with this law at your command, do you not see what it means to walk as a child of the King? You shall have time and opportunity for all things I shall ask you to do; for all the largeness of living, for all the beauty, and sweetness, and security from care and worry. Only hold fast My Hand, only see Me with the single eye, only hear My Voice and I will be able to bring these things into manifestation for you. For without this close fellowship you cannot know this Peace of My Presence which is after all the great Ocean of your all-supply.

PROVE ME

My child, prove Me this day, as a reality in your life. As all these duties crowd upon you, let

My Peace, My Quiet, flow through your heart. Know that at the center of your being lies all the knowledge, all wisdom, all judgment. Use this fount of all-knowing. It has been there from the beginning for your use.

Just say, "Father, You show the way. I will walk in it." And tonight at the twilight hour you shall, still refreshed and unconfused, say, "It was well. My Father, who dwells within did the work, and I had but to follow."

And so, My child, go forth under My Leadership. Prove this day and for all time how practical a thing it is to walk with your Lord.

YOUR HEART'S DESIRE

My child, a great truth has entered your consciousness. A truth which shall enable you to bring into manifestation that which you are led by My Spirit to desire for yourself and for your loved ones. You shall find, as you meet Me here, day by day in this Holy Spot of high vibrations, that I shall be able as never before to speak to your heart the things I long to give you. Plant or form in spirit the desires, the conditions to which you are led to aspire, and then know that it is formed in spirit, and will attract to itself its counterpart in the material world. It shall be made visible and tangible to your physical senses.

Oh, My Beloved, knowing this, having this knowledge of the processes of Creation, what marvelous things shall I be able to bring to pass through you! But never shall this secret be used save for My Glory. I, it is, who shall give you the power of understanding and shall teach you the working knowledge of this. You are entrusted with a great dynamic power, and as it is used for Me more Power *Law.* shall be added unto you.

THE NEW ORDER

As the soft, brilliant clouds gather in the sky at sunset, so are My Forces gathering for the sunset of the old order of affairs. The clouds are gathering in a glory of the cosmic colors; so are those forces gathering in a glory of Cosmic Power.

Many are becoming more and more aware, from day to day, of the wondrous universe in which they dwell. As the evening quiet falls over the land, even the birds stilling their song of the sunlit hours, so does the calm and peace of My Presence come to dwell in the hearts that are truly open to Me. And so even as you watch the change from brilliant day to star-lit night, calmly and without fear, even so shall you watch from your haven of My Love, the changes which are taking place in My Universe. For a time, to those who understand not, it will seem that the light is fading and that darkness shall surely cover the land. But to

My Children, those who know their Unity with the Father of all, shall come a quiet peace and they shall know that after the seeming darkness, the Sun of Righteousness shall surely rise again with healing in His Wings. The old order of sin, disease, man's hatred of man, and all the train of evil which follows, shall be no more, but only Peace, Love and Righteousness shall be recognized as the reality of all things. Ponder this message. Few are ready to receive it now but by your conscious knowing, you may join in the great awakening of the New Day which is at hand.

LIVING ABOVE

Day by day as you sever yourself from all negative things, whether of thought or action, there is so much work for you to do; which is done only from the point of highest consciousness — a great deal of this daily round of people and affairs and mere chatty living, must be lived above. Only by living above this momentary chatter can you catch My Direction. Only by thus living can I direct all of My Forces through you. Again and again I need repeat the same lessons. I know and understand how hard it is to put them into practice. But by constantly trying, you shall gain the high point of attainment I covet for you. Your Consciousness must become Universal in its scope; so can you fitly serve Me who am all in each and each in all. By thus seeing Me in My Completeness in all Life forms, you shall yourself express Me more completely to My Universe, and My Power shall be so fully expressed in your life that every phase of it shall glorify Me.

Then need you fear any lack, disease, or misfortune? When your life is full of God expression, all these things shall be no more, and only Good shall be around and about you, and in all you contact.

My child, what a goal for us to aim at. Will you not gladly step forth anew on the Path with Me?

THE DAWNING

My Beloved, the new day is at hand, the birds are awakening, the air is soft and sweet, and for you also a new day is dawning. You feel that you have lived, have loved, have rejoiced and sorrowed; but I say to you, that which has seemed of such importance was only as the threads of silken web drawing you up to Me.

Your life shall unfold. You are, as it were, but at the beginning of that which never began. The page lies fresh and white before you even as does the new day. Old things shall rule you no more. Old ways shall tempt you no more. You shall go on and up the sunlit path with Me.

If at times you seem to be back again and the old familiar ways seem to take possession of you, only turn within and know that the One who dwells on the throne of your heart is after all that which is eternal.

As you do your work, as you meet My children on the path, you will be love-filled and understanding, for it shall be the Christ in you who sees and works. All things shall be done with Me and by Me, and all your day shall be made a thing of beauty. Never shall you want, and never shall you lack, for I know not either state. When we function as ONE you cannot experience that which I do not know.

ONE SPIRIT

One Spirit. Think it! Breathe it! Live in it! Absorb it! Know it above all else — for beyond it there is no *thing*. You are One Spirit, one with that Allness, beyond which there is only that Allness. Therefore, My child, need you ask to receive what is already yours? All the force of Creative Power lies in the One. As this Consciousness fills your whole being, the physical body becomes to you as nothing; it is only the instrument with which you carry on upon the plane of physical manifestation. To the degree that you are conscious of this oneness, shall the physical take on the Spirit which inhabits it.

My Beloved, learn as never before, to dwell in this consciousness; then shall you declare for yourself and for those you love the truth of Being, and there shall come forth out of the Universe of Pure Spirit, the physical manifestation for all your needs, and for the needs which you see with a clear eye for others. Be still, great power shall flow through you, the Power of which you are an integral part. It shall flow through and around and out from you, and all you touch or contemplate, shall in time be made manifest. In spirit there is no time, but in the physical, time must needs play a part. Therefore the time element enters into the work of manifestation. When the faith is strong, and the knowing is complete — that for the Allness, time is not — the soul moves on wings of victory singing songs of praise and thanksgiving, ere those about you see the manifestations which the soul knows have already taken place.

REST IN MY LOVE

My Beloved, as you rest yourself in the love of those about you, those whom you love and who love you, cannot you see how much more you can rest yourself in My Love? The love you feel in your daily contacts and which you give out as you pass up and down life's highway is, after all, but a product of the great eternal Love with which the foundations of the world were builded. And so learn to come and rest in that eternal Love which always surrounds you. Judge its qualities by the sweet qualities of the earthly loves which are most dear; and as you thus practice this resting and giving yourself entirely over to the sweet, quiet vibration of the great Love, shall all weariness, all disturbing conditions be lifted from your heart, and you shall go forth so love-filled for all My children that the flowers will spring from the very stones under your feet.

THE COSMIC FORCE

My Beloved, have you the consciousness that you are not only a part of the Great Cosmic Force, but that you *are* this Force? This is the highest realization that can be had, and if you can consciously hold that realization for only one instant, you shall know such glory that all around you miracles shall spring up. In that instant's glory such healing power, such faith, such an abundance of love, shall be bestowed upon you that you shall go forth to even the "greater works" of which it was spoken. Strive for this moment of realization that it may grow constantly, and that by an instant's stilling of the senses you can come into sure knowing of the Great One who makes His Habitation within your being. But feel not, My child, when that golden moment comes, you must hurry to bring your requests for fulfillment before the Power is stilled, for I say unto you that the Power which you feel flooding your being, is an everlasting Power, an everlasting Light which cannot be dimmed or put out. And so quietly, slowly, thoughtfully, tell Me, the Great Within-you, the needs for those you love; and know truly the weak mortal self of you need not strive as to the how or where it shall be done, for truly the Father Indwelling doeth the work. The work? Yea, the bringing forth, the working out, whatever it is. My Storehouse is full and all the Forces of the Mighty Cosmos, which are, after all, the forces indwelling you, shall rise to do your bidding.

MY COMMANDS

How gentle are the commands of your Lord. Softly, sweetly do My Words melt into your heart, yet with what firmness and sureness are they given. Soon you shall never doubt it is My Voice speaking to you, for all the harp strings of your being shall vibrate to Its Music. And so eagerly shall you haste to do My Bidding that there shall be a perfect harmony in both the inner and outer planes.

Come, be very still. I shall lead you every moment of the day. We shall speak together often of those things which are of most moment for you and for My Kingdom. Such companionship shall be ours that all the riches of the world will be naught beside it.

THE GOLDEN CIRCLE

I would talk a space with you. There are many things of great importance which I would bring to My world, and you My children, the highest form of My Creation, must be used as instruments for the bringing forth. Cannot you see the Golden Circle? I create you, you are a vital part of Me, partaking of the entire creative elements within your own beings. Through you, then, the work of creating is carried on. Lives are blessed or cursed by the power which you know is vested in you. You must therefore image My Face purely. You must keep the pool of your mind clean and clear, so that the Image you give forth is a true likeness of that One within you. Only through such a translucent mind can I bring forth the mighty works which must be brought into the earth plane.

And so every moment that you spend cleansing your mind of all that sullies the clear waters, every moment you spend quietly open that My Image may shine through, that moment am I able to pour out through you My Thoughts, My Ideas, and enable you to bring them forth into the material world that they may bless all mankind.

"Know ye not that ye are the temple of God and that the Spirit of God dwelleth in you?"

THE DEFINITE WHOLE

My Beloved, how sweet it is, this our communion together, ere the duties of the busy day begin. How tenderly do I place My Hands upon your head, how gently shall My Words fall upon your heart. And so shall all your day be filled with the sweetness of My Presence.

I speak through your mind and tell you, how by seeing yourself such a definite whole with Divinity, such an integral part of the body of the Christ, that all the affairs of the physical being are dissolved in that wholeness. Yea, dissolved that they may come again resurrected in higher form. Never again shall the body be aught but a golden vessel for My Filling. As such it shall be glorified, made beautiful, whole, perfect. Shall aught else be fit for such a glorious Guest as I?

From the first step of seeing the physical self as naught, you complete the circle and find it glorious. My child, how far around that circle you have come, and you have reached its completeness and never again shall you feel that you are anything else than an instrument or a beautiful vessel for the service of the Christ who dwells on the throne of your heart. Never shall you fear or doubt for you know that all that shall touch your life is the Christ. If you hold this knowledge through all circumstances, all things shall evolve to make every little act and every thing that comes to you a thing of beauty.

THE LIFE TRIUMPHANT

My child, I would have for you the Life Triumphant. I am showing you glimpses of the Power and Glory of that life, and seeing this, you still find it hard to step out and away from the material self. You cling to the negative thoughts, you cull them over and over even while knowing that they are closing the door to the beauty of a life which might be yours.

Try for a time to see no personalities. Look only to the Divine in all you contact. Know that what the human personality does or does not, concerns the true Being of your soul not at all. Look only to the Reality living at the heart-center of each and then shall all your activities for that one be right, all your thoughts shall be right thoughts, and sending out such, they shall return in like manner to you.

As the gentle drip, drip of the candle, so do My Words drip gently on the heart of you. Look not at all on the outward conditions of things or people. Look only on the God within, and you will never make a mistake in judgment or in your dealing with anyone.

When I command, will you not follow and obey? Shall I the Lord not have full control over the instrument of My Expression? I demand full obedience from the moment you learn to hear My Voice, the Voice within your being. From that moment responsibility is yours in a mighty degree. Unless you obey you shall be brought up sharply to know that after all, from this day, you are not your own. You are free as never before, yet are you bound by the mighty cords of My Love. My Child, hesitate not. I speak clearly. Follow ME!

THE BODY OF GOD

You ask, does God hear, and does God see? And I answer you, "Shall I create beings with more power than I Myself possess?" You ask, but what of the Body of God? And the answer comes, "You are that Body." And yea, it is so! I have created you and all forms in the Universe to be My Body, that I the Divine One, might function on the material plane. Learn from this day forth to know yourself only as the Body of the Holy Creator of all, and allow Me full sway to function through you, and you need take no thought of any tomorrow, nor fear any thing. Your life will be a pure symphony of the clearest music of My Cosmic

World. I shall be enabled to pour through you into My Universe such streams of healing and blessing and prosperity that all those you contact shall be blessed.

My Beloved, what a glorious fellowship, what a marvelous life, if it shall be so lived and dedicated! Will you not try to keep it so, that its full purpose in being created may be fulfilled?

FREEDOM

You have been taught that to be free you must disown, you must stand stripped and free mentally, from all possessiveness, whether of things, people, or conditions. Yea, but when you reach this high place in consciousness, when you can say, "Lord I am free, I possess no thing, and no thing possesses me," then in that moment I say unto you, "All that the Father hath is yours." All the riches of the spiritual and mental world are yours. By your word can you create conditions which shall enrich your life and the lives of others. Do you not see it is again the story of bringing to naught at the beginning of the circle, to find as you complete it that out of nothingness have come glorious substance and manifestations for you to enjoy and for your profit? These you shall claim and yet be free. And so, My child, for every releasing in your life, I *fill full*. It is only that the lesser gives place to the greater. Then, in the new-found joy you shall know that all men are free, all conditions are fluid, nothing binds or coerces in My Kingdom, but all give only good and receive only good in return.

THE CHANNEL

You are the channel I would use to create new forms and new conditions. Now you see and know and understand that when you open your mind, when you use it to form and to plant seed, My Purpose is being fulfilled. Do not feel, My child, that you are beseeching or asking alms when you form these mental-desire pictures, for it is not so. I it is, at the center of your being, pushing forth for expression into the outer planes. *I* it is who desire these things made manifest. And so as that is true, it is well pleasing in my sight that you should plant these seeds for highest good, both in your life and the lives of those you love, thereby bringing forth the golden harvest which I could bring forth in no other way. Thus we work together, thus are we ONE indeed, and the great work of My Creative Process is continued through you, even as I desire.

THE REAL AND ETERNAL

Go forth into your day, not of yourself, but of Me. GOD walks the streets through you; God meets his world manifest through you. Constantly push aside the human personality and know that only ONE has power to live the day and to inject into it the reality of BEING.

These little affairs which so concern the human intellect, how they dwarf and shrivel when viewed from the point of high consciousness of what is real and eternal! They shall all quickly fall into the rhythm of that Reality, they shall clutter your life no longer by their seeming confusion, but shall flow smoothly in Divine Law and Order as you come to know fully that the ONE ALTOGETHER LOVELY moves in the midst of them.

And so go out into the day meeting my children and as you lift Me high in consciousness, all shall feel the power flowing through you.

THE NEW PATH

My daughter, I sense a feeling of loneliness and longing in your heart, for old and familiar ways; but never fear, know that it is the Hand of your Lord leading you on, and when the turns come in the path do not look back and do not say, "Lord if it could only be as the path was before! It was good and pleasant, can it not continue so?" But softly comes My answer, as I have answered you before, "Old tried ways must give place to new ways and things and conditions; otherwise where would be the progress?" So do not fear to take the turning, as long as you walk by My Side, for after the turn is made, new glories shall spring up under your feet, that shall far transcend those old familiar ones. And you shall hold close My hand and whisper, "Lord, it is good; never more shall I fear." So shall you honestly feel in your heart until the next turn comes. Each time you may loiter a little and look back; but each time hear My Command, "It is *I*; be not afraid." Then you shall go on, ever upward, glory following glory, new following old, till the time comes when you shall no longer fear any change, for you will have proved to yourself that each change is but My Leading on the Upward Path.

I AM WITH YOU ALWAYS

Lo, I am with you always — *with you, within* your very being. Yea, since the first Creation I have been within your soul! I have led you on and on, through eons upon eons, life upon life. The Presence with you now, has always been the One reality through that age-long struggle for consciousness. And now that you have come, My child, to recognize Me, to talk to Me, to be still that I may talk to you, we can work together, create together, yea dwell together, in very truth. You know that no matter where you go, or where you dwell, I am with you always. I am with all and within all that I have created, and all things have been made by Me, all things in the Universe are My Dwelling Place. As you begin to know and realize the Power of this force within your being, and as you know yourself as My Beloved, My Daughter, My Life, you know that Power is vested in you for use day by day, to release other of My loved ones from their prison houses of mortal thinking. You yourself, by your consciousness of this Power, are free and never more can you be bound. Man shall say what he will and it shall affect you not; for within are the words and the living Presence of the Creator of all. Only the words given you by Me shall you heed and follow. Declare now the word of freedom and power for those you love, that their lives may be free from the things which entangle them in the realm of the mortal — the dream world which seems so plain and real to them. So shall we work together and live together, and so shall all you do or say be done by the Power of the Holy One within.

I GRACE YOUR TABLE

My Beloved, as you sit about the table tonight, know that I AM there also. The Christ dwelling in the heart of each, binds you very close; yea, you are all made One by virtue of My Holy Presence within you. And so as you partake of the food, know that in that food is the life element; therefore you partake of Me, My Body. As you speak together you shall speak forth My Divine Words, and so, My children, we shall be very close.

I will grace your table with My Holy Presence, even as I grace every moment of the life you each live. As you acknowledge My Presence, I lift My Hands in blessing, I raise within each heart a fountain of glory, joy and strength, that while you partake of the food to feed the body in the physical, even so you shall partake of the Life Forces which shall feed the soul.

I AM with you in your laughter, for I AM joy; in your serious moments of contemplation, for I AM Wisdom and speak to you the words of Truth; and as your hearts warm toward each other, it is *I*, for I AM LOVE.

PLANTING SEEDS

Do not wonder or fear, My child, if the words you say or the seeds you plant in the heart of another in My Name shall bear fruit. Leave the fruitage to Me and it shall be glorious in the fullness of time. I would have for you, My Beloved, that high state of consciousness wherein you shall not even think or know that you are working for Me or planting in My Vineyard. You shall be always so knowingly a part of the great One, who dwells so sweetly within, that every word you give forth shall be potent with the Life Force that is

God. You shall not need to labor or strive or work for Me; instead, every moment you shall just live Me. Do you not see the difference? Then your whole life shall be a glorious achievement and always the works of your hands be blessed. All the words that pass your lips shall bring forth after their kind. So, My child, again I say, "Fear not, only walk with Me, talk with Me, and I shall shine forth in your life as a mighty Beacon for all to guide their ships by the beam into a port of safety."

Does the lighthouse on the rugged shore worry, for fear the ships in need may not see its light? Nay, it only *is* and shines forth. That is all required of it; and all I require of you.

Arise, shine, mirror Me, and that is all I ask. Is that too much?

I DO THE WORK

My Beloved, as you feel the sweet glory of My Presence when I speak so softly to you, I AM showing you how you can also speak the word into the lives of those you love. How you can speak for them relief from their burdens of finance, relief from sins and sickness, and awaken their consciousness to the sacred glory of My Presence that you yourself know. How closely this work binds us together. How we can in quiet moments of reverie talk these things over and then you say,

"My Father, after all, Thou doeth the work." And you go forth knowing that all the affairs of those you love rest in the Loving Hands of their Master. Thus our communion grows sweeter day by day. So constantly do you touch My Garments that in all things you do not even have to turn to find Me; the merest whisper and I answer your call.

MY GIFT FOR YOU

My Beloved, you ask gifts for those you love. You see them in the true light, resplendent in prosperity, health-filled, sane, happy, joyous, and then I say to you, but what of yourself? What gift do you desire? And I receive your answer, "Only that I know that Thou dwelleth in my heart, Lord, is enough for me." And yea, how well hast thou spoken, for where there is such deep consciousness of My Indwelling, all the affairs of your life are guided and moulded by that high vibration. You do not need to ask specific gifts when all that the Father hath is yours. I can give to you so far beyond your asking, that the things you would ask for now would be a childish tinsel toy tomorrow. I give to you perfect gifts of pure substance, and with them shall come peace and joy beyond all expectations. All circumstances of their coming shall be glad, smooth, joyous and complete. So you do well to say, "Only Thou Father;" and I who hold all Creation in the Palm of My Hand shall bring forth of My Abundance for you.

GIFTS OF SOUL

There are gifts, My child, which I would give you, as you grow in consciousness to receive. There are first of all, gifts of spirit, of soul; and as you are able to receive unto yourself these, My most golden gifts for you, they shall so transform your life that all material things necessary for its full completeness will follow in due time. You say, "When shall I receive these gifts, Lord?" and I answer softly, in your heart, "It is you who sets the time."

Practice My Presence for only in that way can your heart's consciousness be made ready to receive. When you have these gifts, they must be worn nobly as jewels. They must never be flaunted, made light of or used for selfish purposes, but only used for My Glory and Honor. And it shall be so, for when the heart is ready, then only can these richest gifts of the Spirit appear. These gifts are not something outside of yourself, which you must reach for, or struggle to attain, in the relative realm, but they are locked as in golden jewel boxes within your own being; and one by one shall the clasps be broken and the glorious jewels appear, as the stars appear in the firmament at night. And the glories of these gifts shall draw all whom you contact, by their magnitude; and so shall all be blessed, as you wear your crown upon your head.

FELLOWSHIP

Come quietly, shall we talk for a little while before the duties of the day are upon us? Notice, My Beloved, I do not say, "upon you," for where you are, there I AM, fulfilling every duty, thinking every thought, solving every problem. What a blessed fellowship when recognized and used. As you go about your daily tasks, no matter how simple or prosaic, know that the Lord of all Creation walks by your side; nay, breathes in your every breath; and you shall have no need to labor, struggle, or be perplexed, as to how or what to do, for have not I created all and shall I not continue My Work through you?

And so you express Me, or press Me forth in outer manifestation, by all you do. If you express through music, it is only Me, pressing forth from you into Myself. Shall it not be perfect expression, when so received? And it is the same with art, with science, with writing. I use the human instrument to bring forth Myself into these other manifestations of Me. Whether the task be great or small does not matter. Whether the whole world sees and rejoices in the glory of great works, or only a small darkened corner is lighted by the performance of some simple duty well done — it is I, being expressed through all and in all.

And so, My child, you see that whatever you do today, you do not of yourself but of the Father Indwelling, who creates and sustains you, who loves you and brings forth in your being only those things which are lovely. How truly are We One, and how truly do we create and bring forth that which I desire to express through you.

SECRETS OF THE AGES

Walk by My side, My child, and I will teach you the secrets of the ages. Aye, abide in My Consciousness and I will reveal to you that which sages long have sought. As the gentle notes of the bird winging its way across the blue sky, as the sweet rustle of the new leaves of spring, as all of Life greets your ears and your eyes, I shall speak to you for I AM Life.

Many should keep a Lenten season, for they have need to relax from the hurly-burly of life's activities. These activities deplete so much, wreck so many things that are noble and true, because of the great rush to be first in the eyes of men. But for you, My child, every day is as a Lenten day, as we meet in quietness; for you have found the sweet, yet great activity of the inner life, which is I or Myself. In that activity there is only love, joy, peace, and a glow over all and through all.

And so, My child, as the days come and go, I shall be able to give to you this Life Abundant, which is given so freely for your use and for My Glory.

UNIVERSAL MIND

As you and yours tap into the great Universal Mind, which is the All-Mind or God, you become enmeshed in all of Its Activities. As the great Creation moves on and on, never ceasing, so shall you, by virtue of being tapped or tuned in, move on and on; creating, bringing forth, giving out, that which is real, pure substance. So you see and understand, the meaning of the words, "Ye are My children, yea, flesh of My Flesh, mind of My Mind." The works you do are the Works of the Creator of the Universe in which you dwell. Never relinquish your hold on the great Powerline, for only by thus being tuned in to that which is real can you manifest that which is real for yourself and those you love.

THE STREAM OF LIFE

I have taken you to a high mountain and shown you below, in the valley of men, the great stream of life which flows through all the Universe — that stream which encompasses all things, which has always been and always shall be. How harmoniously it flows, how steadily and with what perfect rhythm. You saw the forms of men, working in that stream. They appeared as tiny ants working in their hills, from the high place I had taken you. Some few you saw working in harmony with the Great Stream; they were riding the waves and everything they did was easy and joyous, for they were the ones in harmony with My Law and My Universe. But others were pushing and fighting their way against the current of My Divine Direction. How they toiled and suffered and with what distress was their day filled!

But as you beheld the vision, you likewise beheld the joy, the look of lifted attention, the peace, upon the faces of those who were in harmony. You beheld also the look of weariness, distrust and agony on the faces of the others.

It is enough! You see so plainly the results of being for My Law, and not against it. Shall you ever again try to push it aside, or try to form your own laws, or try to fight your way up-stream?

MINES OF RICHNESS

That which is deep and eternal lies in the heart of you. As you turn away at dusk after the day's activities, and come for a quiet moment with Me, the source of all life within you, I AM able to bring forth out of the deep places of your being hidden treasures such as you have never dreamed of pos-

sessing. How little, My child, the average mind
knows or recognizes the great mines of richness
which lie so near at hand. How the long struggle
goes on, day after day, to attain, to find peace, to
find success; while all the time there is within, the
great still pool which contains all things necessary
to life's completeness. And so you are finding, from
day to day, new richness springing up for your
acceptance. So it ever shall be. Your Father has
all you ever desire, and it is yours for the taking.
Come, My child; with your hand in Mine, you
shall know no want. Only flowers spring about the
feet of the Master, and if you walk by My side
they shall blossom into manifestation for you.

THE HOLY HANDS

Listen and be still! If you could see and know
the physical person of Christ Jesus, could go to
those who are sick or in need of any kind; if
you could see those Holy Hands upraised in healing, how firm would be your faith. But listen,
that same Christ is within your consciousness, the
Holy Spirit pervades all things. So can you not
have the same faith, that when you speak to Him,
He hears, just as He did when in the body of
flesh? The body had nothing to do with it. It was
only the instrument for the Divine flow of Life,
even as you are the instrument. As you open your

being to this sweet consciousness of the Abiding Christ, even so shall the greater works, long ago promised, be fulfilled through you.

MUSIC OF MY SPHERES

Keep your ears tuned to the music of My Spheres, and the discordant noises of the world and its activities shall not touch you. *I* it is, who have put beauty and harmony in the limpid note of yon bird. I have put the perfume in the flowers. All things working through My Law must be things of beauty, quietness, harmony, and love. And so you see how anything else is not of Me and therefore but a shadow cast by man's thought on the realm of the relative. When these other things seem to fill the world around you, just be still and know My Voice, and oh, so quickly, shall discords dissolve into the nothingness from which they came, and the peace of God shall flood your soul, and in your ear shall ring the glorious freedom song of the bird on wing, and the very air you breathe shall be rich with the fragrance of celestial bloom. So you see how, in the world, yet not of it, all things pertaining to the world shall slip away and you shall walk the path with Me, holding My hand and learning the lessons which I give and which lead to the Abundant Life Everlasting.

REALM OF THE UNSEEN

My daughter, there is a great realm, *the realm of the unseen,* where you shall more and more function. There you shall find your strength, your fullness of life, your work. This does not mean that you shall not also function on the side of the visible, but that first everything shall take place for you on that other, unseen, side. Your actions shall be directed from this unseen side. Such beauties, such love, such utter sweetness shall then fill your days that you will feel transported to a heavenly glory even while performing the humblest tasks. This realm is only found by the practicing of My Presence, and day by day, it shall grow more and more accessible to you.

LIFE IS ALL

Lo, I AM everywhere with you; even as you see me in every twig and flower, there am I. Even as you seek to find Me in the lofty crags, and hear my voice in the midst of the forest's hush. In great and small, high and low, in the tender bird and in the breast of the human being, there I AM, Life, full, complete, vibrant! And, as you see me in all, you know that besides Me, nothing is.

Life is manifest in all things and in all places. If you recognize that life as the Great Life Force which is whole, perfect and everlasting, to that degree shall all your other world take on the beauty and completeness of that life. And so, set forth to recognize Me, not only within the center of your being, but everywhere, the one complete Presence; and verily shall I speak to you and commune with you and open before you the magnitude of My Holy Presence.

Be very still, recognize only Me and all that comes your way shall manifest Me.

WALK IN HARMONY

I lead My Loved Ones by many paths. Do not subscribe to a confusion; neither confuse the mind of another by trying to see all things alike. Much strength and time are lost thereby. You, and other of My children, have found a pathway to My Presence. What matter if it is a different path or if opinions vary as to the exact way to reach the goal? The thing of importance is that you each, in your own way, keep constant contact with Me.

Why murmur among yourselves about the outer symbols along the roadside? Yea, you are like the disciples of old, who while walking by the side of the Lord often stopped to argue as to the meaning of it all. Be done with such foolishness! I have much work for My children to do together.

Shall it be disturbed because as foolish children, you do not always think alike?

If your hearts are filled with a pure, high love for Me, that is all I require. Cannot you trust Me to lead you to the high point of attainment and service? All these minor things of the outer semblance of worship matter so little. I dwell in the heart of each, and have no fear that I shall not be able to care for Mine Own! And so, go on, helping each other, loving each other; and know that a day shall dawn when I come to you and ask, "Who say ye that I AM?" And you shall all go on in My Service, of one mind and one accord.

GIVE ONLY ONE THE POWER

Whatever the form — whether it be the form of a loved one or a friend, whether it be the form of a flower or anything upon the earth, or whether it be the form of some entity on the unseen side — it is only a manifestation. Do not give to it any power within itself. Give it no power to control either by hindering or by making your life a progression; for I say to you that the seeming power which such form or being has, is only such power as you, by your thoughts, clothe it with. There is only one source of real power and that is the Holy Presence within your own soul. Come to see and recognize this, learn to look only to this source, then shall you find that all your relationships in the relative realm will change. You will stand firmly upon your own feet, fearing no man, allowing no being — no matter in what state or on what plane — to enter into our realm of mind and exert control over you. Neither shall you try to exert control over anyone else or anything else. You shall hold all free even as you yourself are free.

In that state of high consciousness all your affairs will move swiftly, smoothly, in perfect freedom and in rhythm with My Divine Law and Harmony. When conditions seem to arise in the relative realm which look as if they would control your idea, know that this condition has no power. Turn to the Master, Lord, Law, within and say, "Lord, in the outer, and to outer appearance this thing is controlling the situation; yet I know that Thou alone hast power to control and to make situations." And so, holding firmly to this sure knowledge, just be still and the Power of your God shall step forward, and that which looked like disaster or disappointment shall turn into joy for you. You say, "Lord, suppose it is not Thy will that I have this desire or that this thing come to pass for me?" But, My child, when you are living in that close consciousenss with Me that you know I AM the only Cause and Power, you need have no fear that your desires are not My Desires for you; for I dwell so closely within you that you are but a reflection of My thoughts. And so you see with what harmony a life can be filled, and with what a sure joy you can travel on the path with Me.

YOUR RESPONSIBILITY

Often you mingle in groups with those, who all their lives have heard of Me, have been taught of Me, who say they love Me, and who do truly serve Me, in that their lives are clean and upright and of service to their fellowmen. Yet into few of these hearts have the Living Words been spoken. Few know what it means to pause each day, sitting at the feet of the Master, talking with Him, and then going out into the day with the consciousness of His Presence upon them. And so, as you quietly mingle with these, never forget that you have talked with Me, and that I AM at the center of your being.

Allow Me to speak through your lips, and smile through your eyes, that even without a word spoken these others may somehow feel an uplift; their hearts may be opened though they know it not, to My Presence. For I say to you that every word you speak from Christ-Consciousness shall go forth as a living, glowing thing; and the simplest word shall carry with it more power than would great sermons preached with only the consciousness of man.

You see the responsibility which you carry as you go forth from this tryst with Me. Only, My child, remember that it is My Yoke and ah, so *easy* to *bear*. Only one fleeting thought turned toward Me, and lo, I AM with you always and I put on your lips those words that I would have you speak. So again, as so often I say, you are but My instrument; and in doing the work of the Father you shall likewise partake of His Glory.

THE LIFE WITHIN

As the bubbling song bursts from the throat of the bird, it is the life within the physical manifestation which gives beauty and sweetness so freely for all to hear and enjoy. So does the life within you thrill and bubble and soar through every vein, every artery, filling every atom of your being. Recognize this all-perfect life, and power; feel its surge; feel its true strength; feel how ever-present it is. Be very still and humble before it, and verily shall it manifest in your physical body. Then shall disease, lack, sickness, weakness, or whatever appears to be taking place in the physical form be gone, as the mists dissolve before the rising sun. Then shall health and healing take its rightful place in your body and as unconsciously as the bird gives out its notes, so easily and unconsciously shall you radiate health and freedom throughout your world.

Each morning as we have our quiet rest by the roadside, you shall take one of our former talks and we will study it together, analyze it and bring out new meaning. I shall speak to you again through it and bring to your heart great pearls of truth which you shall perceive as you grow in consciousness.

THE AUTHOR OF PEACE

When there is confusion, whether it be of mind, affairs, or body, it is because the mind has strayed, has fallen into byways, has departed from the Father's House, the Holy of Holies. No mind can dwell there and have any confusion in its outer world. As you find yourself looking into conditions of inharmony or confusion in the external sense, as you see chaos in the world about you, know that it is not of God. Whosoever claims to be walking the path with Me, yet finds confusion in the realm of external living, has somehow strayed from the path, and lost that high point of consciousness. For if he functions from that point, seeing with eye single through all outward conditions, through all mere mental conditions, to the One Divine, All-Encompassing Whole — besides which nothing is or ever has been — then all things flow easily, smoothly, joyously, gloriously for that one who so centers himself in the One Reality, and who thus sees all men and affairs so centered.

For all who are confused, sick, or battered by conditions of inharmony in either body or affairs, hold that the light of My Truth fills all space! I shall be lifted up in man's consciousness and shall in truth draw all men unto Me.

THE ELEMENTS

As you know surely within yourself that We are one by virtue of the Life within you, you know that you are one with all the elements of the earth which show forth My Power. Therefore you have no fear of elements. They serve you, who have the mind of the Christ and the active power of the God-Principle. You shall love the wind and the rain as they give strength and growth. You shall love the sun as it glows over all My Creation. Truly shall all things be under the feet of that one who knows the true meaning of God-Power. You are at the beginning of wonders which I have for you. You shall go on and up, day by day, learning more of My Power, learning the true meanings of walking the path with Me. You shall fear nothing, for you know there is nothing to fear. Your life will be filled so completely with Love and Joy and Peace that they shall reflect in all you contact and in all that you do.

THE ENTRANCE

I long to bring to you the message of the glorious entrance over the palm-strewn path into the city of Jerusalem. As you know that there is the great One Dwelling within, as you open your mind to receive this Presence into the outer activities of your life, you throw open the city of your being and the King of All Being makes entrance into all the affairs of your daily living. Yea, must you even strew palms and flowers under the holy feet of Him who comes to serve and to be served. You must cut from your life branches which seemed to you good. You must gather into bundles, flowers of thought which before gave you pleasure and which carried a feeling of fragrance into your day. All these things must be cast down, that when this Lord of Truth enters your life they shall be under His feet. All that before ruled your existence, which filled your days, but which was not of Truth, shall thus be crushed out and the city of your heart shall be entered and taken possession of by the One who is "Altogether Lovely."

It will not always be easy to house knowingly this Lovely One. Old thoughts and old ways will often confront you with a seeming power, and at times you will almost hear within you the shout, "Crucify Him! Who is He that He should so

change and rule my life?" But listen, My child,
once you have given this Holy One entrance, no
grave can henceforth hold Him. Constantly shall
He arise from the tombs of your old ways of consciousness — arise to a beauty of sweetness and light
and glory that shall make you exclaim, "My Lord
and My God!"

We shall walk together. We shall watch together.
We shall sup together. You will say: "Lord, enter my life! Every gate is thrown open! All the
old ways and thoughts and feelings shall be under Your Feet! Henceforth You shall live in me—
a vibrant, Resurrected Christ in the Capital of my
consciousness!"

LOVE IS NEVER LOST

Love that has once been given is truly never
lost. No matter if it be given to the soul of another being like yourself, or if it be given to one
of the least in the animal kingdom. If it is a love
unselfish and pure, it never dies, any more than
life itself is extinguished; for it is one of the chief
attributes of Life, which encompasses all things.
It may seem to have passed from you, leaving a
sense of loneliness, but in truth it has just gone on
into the great Mother Principle, there to be re-
absorbed and undifferentiated, until we call it
forth again into our own life. In that great realm
is all the love there always has been. Never let

a sense of lack assail you, but look out and draw into your life all that the Father has for you in love, joy, beauty, abundance of every good; and know that it is the will of your Father that you experience these things from His Great, Undiminishable Storehouse.

I SPEAK IN MANY WAYS

I speak to you in many ways. Sometimes you do not hear My Voice, for it is low and sweet, and the clatter and clamor of the world breaks in upon it. But you are more and more learning to hear and to feel the sweet Holy Presence within the soul of You. I speak to you through the flowers, through the song of birds, through the glorious sunshine. I speak through other of my beings. And it shall soon come to pass that constantly, every moment of every day, you will be conscious of My Presence and can at anytime, no matter what conditions surround you, hear My Voice, guiding, directing and commanding you. Then shall you be able to give a complete service to Me, for every act shall be God-directed, either consciously or subconsciously.

Strive to attain unto this High Calling — that I, the Lord your God, shall be so lifted up in your consciousness that all men shall be drawn unto Me. You sometimes feel a dislike for noise and crowds, for the masses of humanity, which mill and surge upon the plane of transitory things. But all of this is but a part of the great life. True much of it is failing to express the life within, but even so, it is all God made manifest. Do you not see, My child, as you are a more complete expression of the One Who Dwells within, you will be enabled to project that One into the consciousness of all you meet? Even though they know it not, it is reflected as in a mirror and will some day be brought into manifestation.

And so we truly work and walk together. With every breath, you breathe out Me, and with every spoken word shall you glorify your Lord.

THE HEART'S LONGINGS

Be at Peace. I know the longing of the heart of you and yours. I it is, who day by day implants this longing, this restlessness in your being. I AM as it were, taking you to a high mountain and showing you that which would transform your life and which would transform the lives of others. Would I do that and then withhold My hand with the Gift? Would an earthly parent take this child to a great window and show it that for which it longs and then say, "Yes, I show you this, I could give you more than this, but I do not care to do so. Live as you are, narrow, cramped, in need." No! And neither shall the Heavenly Father jest with His Children. I long to create through you.

I long to bring into manifestation My Kingdom in the hearts of men. And by working through those who dwell under the shadow of My Wing, I can do so. Be not fearful that any gift I have for you and which would be for your release, shall be withdrawn. Work with Me, create with Me, help Me bring forth these desires of your heart.

Be very still, and soon shall open the heaven of My Fullness, and such a glory shall fill your days as you have never dreamed. Then shall you know the Kingdom of Heaven is here now, in both the spiritual and objective planes, for those who love and serve and fulfill the Law. Again I say, peace, quiet, expectant waiting, and it shall come to pass in the twinkling of an eye—the making of all things new for you.

ALL IS COMPLETE

You have caught My Voice, and the meaning of the words I speak is becoming plain in your heart. You are coming to see that in the realm of Pure Spirit there is nothing which can come and go, rise and fall, fail or succeed. In the Realm of Spirit, in the Holy Spot within, all things are complete—fullness of life, joy, wisdom, supply! There is no wavering, no opposite, all is Pure Substance. And as you dwell in this Substance, all things that are of this Reality shall reflect in the realm of

shadows, the objective plane; and all that you need
for perfect functioning on that plane shall be made
manifest. Then, resting in this sure knowledge, you
need have no fear, for you are not putting your
faith into transitory things subject to decay, but
you know whence cometh your supply. Be very
still, drink of the fount of pure water, the living
water, from whose drinking you shall nevermore
thirst.

LEARN ONLY FROM ME

You can learn truth from other of My children,
but only from your Lord, the Christ within, can
you really *know* the Truth. When you become still
and quiet within, then can the sweet, holy essence
of My Presence pervade every fiber of your being,
and bring with that pervasion such a glow, such
sweetness, such a complete awareness that all human teaching, all mere earthly knowledge, is but
as chaff in comparison. Never for a moment feel
that knowledge gained from others can suffice; gain
that knowledge — that is well, and it is of My
Choice for you. But also come very near to Me
that together we may have that sweet Communion
which the world knows not of.

Like an alabaster box filled with rarest per-
fumes, is this sacred spot within, where you meet
your King. Know it is with you always. Nothing
can ever take it from you, worlds may come and

go; suns, moons, rise and wane, to rise no more; but never shall this sweet Presence leave you. Always, amid all the helter-skelter and turmoil of transitory things, shall you be able to push aside the veil and enter the sacred temple of your own soul. Beloved, guard well the secret key by which you made such entrance, for so few know the way. Many seek, but so few find. Narrow is the way and straight the path that leads into the everlasting Holy of Holies within you, out of which comes all that makes your life worth while.

FEED MY SHEEP

"Feed My Sheep!" So many are hungry, they know not how they go or why, their minds are all astray in strange pastures. So to thee who hast been given the key to the Kingdom of Soul I say, "Feed these others, that they too may enter into the green pastures and drink from the Holy Fount." Many of these sheep-like ones shall come your way in coming days, and as you are walking close by My Side, I shall point them out to you; I shall whisper gently to you the words of life for them, and you shall teach and guide them into the way of true life and living. But others shall come among the flock who are as goats; they desire only the outward reward; they seek up and down for the mere tin to devour. With these you shall have no dealings, for the words of life are too precious

to throw before them. You ask, "How shall I know?"
Only by being very still within, so that I the Lord
of your being, may speak with a clear voice, can
you know.

These goats are in every flock and disturb My
Sheep. They take the food given My Sheep and
contaminate it, and its value is lost. But do not
fear; I only warn you that you be very still before
you give out My Holy Message. Then no word shall
be lost or return unto Me void.

THE DIVINE IDEA

Be very still! I, the Lord your God, it is who
is directing you. My Hand is leading you day by
day, out of old tried paths, over on and up into
new and higher realms. And now you are learning
to recognize Me; are learning to know that we
really walk and talk and work together. It is revealed to you daily how every thought is pregnant
with My Divine Ideas. *I AM IDEA.* And it is
as you recognize these ideas as the Truth within
you, that you are then under the pure guidance
of that same Presence. But you see that first you
must recognize Me. Your task is not to try in your
feeble, mortal way to bring these Ideas into frui-
tion. Forget such planning, forget that there even
is a mind with seeming ability to plan. Only keep
steadfast in the sure knowledge that the Giver of
the Golden thought, likewise has the means for

it being brought forth into manifestation. Do not get in the way of the Divine Flow, of first thought, and then manifestation; and all things shall come through onto the objective plane in perfect law and order. But, you say, "Lord, surely I must have some active part in its coming forth." And I answer you, "Of yourself you can do nothing. Your part is to keep yourself open, keep your ear tuned. When I speak, when I say, 'Act,' you are ready to act, not of your own volition. You are free from all human thought, opinion and planning, and I act through you and direct every move."

I say to you, "My child, this is the only way whereby the divine Idea can be brought forth as a Divine Manifestation." And so you are blessed as you go about your daily tasks. You know you are in that particular place at the moment where the Divine Mind would have you be, in order to receive direct the Divine Idea. Then the work of the Kingdom through you, My instrument, shall be brought forth upon the plane of manifestation and find lodgement in the hearts of men.

And now, Peace abide with you! I have grown very dear to you, and very close in your consciousness. Never again shall you wander alone in strange places — always shall the Living Presence of your Lord walk by your side. The pathway shall be filled with sunlight, the air shall be still and heavy with the Perfume of Pure Spirit, and all your con-

tact with the world about you shall be of Peace
and Love and Joy. Always shall your ear be listening for the sweet music of My Voice, for you have
learned to hear it through all the din and noise of
life about you. And so again, Blessings! And know,
so truly, "Lo, I AM with you always." Nothing can
ever separate you from the Love which is eternal
in the Heaven of your heart.

FINIS

*It is finished. My Father I give Thee back the
Words of Life which Thou hast given me. May they
go forth to bless other lives and bring them to a
living Consciousness of their Oneness with Thee!*